The GRAND RIVER
An Aerial Journey

The GRAND RIVER
An Aerial Journey

GRAND RIVER CONSERVATION FOUNDATION
PHOTOGRAPHY AND TEXT BY CARL HIEBERT
Foreword by The Honourable Lincoln M. Alexander

National Library of Canada Cataloguing in Publication

Hiebert, Carl, 1947-
   The Grand River : an aerial journey / Carl Hiebert.

ISBN 0-9683389-3-3

1. Grand River Watershed (Ont.) — Aerial photographs.
I. Grand River Conservation Foundation II. Title.

FC3095.G72H48 2003   971.3'404'0222   C2003-903292-2
F1059.G78H54 2003

Grand River Conservation Foundation
400 Clyde Rd.
Cambridge, Ontario N1R 5W6

Printed in Canada by Friesens, Altona, Manitoba
First Printing: October 2003
Second Printing: October 2004

PRODUCTION TEAM:

Editor - Ralph Beaumont
Research - David Schultz, Barbara Veale, Warren Yerex, Martin Neumann, Tracey Ryan, Anne Loeffler, Warren Stauch
Designer - Gillian Stead
Map Design - Lara Vujanic

ON THE COVER: *Grand Valley*
PAGE 7: *The Nith River near Wellesley*

ACKNOWLEDGMENTS

Many hands have shaped this book. My grateful thanks to:

Friends who shared the front of their aircraft for the best view:
   Ed Lubitz, Tom Jeary, Steve Gingerich, Perry Weber, Paul Ernest

Kerry Wilkinson for allowing me to fly from York Field.

Many people who shared their stories for my captions.

Warren Stauch and Barbara Veale, for research assistance.

Kim Morouney, for your creative talent in caption rewriting.

Abdul Alarakhia at B&J Photo, for consistent processing

Gill Stead - my designer, and simply the best.

The Grand River Conservation Foundation, in particular, Ralph Beaumont, for the vision to do this book.

It's been my good fortune to work with all of you.

Carl Hiebert

SC Johnson

A FAMILY COMPANY

Dedicated to

S. C. Johnson & Son, Limited

of Brantford, Ontario

by the Grand River Conservation Foundation

for more than twenty years of partnering

on important environmental projects

that benefit residents

of the Grand River Watershed

THE
GRAND RIVER
WATERSHED

The GRAND RIVER

An Aerial Journey

WINTERBOURNE — *Every year, for a few mornings in late summer, I am treated to mesmerizing "steam fog" along lakes and rivers. The water has reached its maximum seasonal temperature while the land, with shorter days, begins to cool. By nightfall, the river is a warm moisture source for the cooling air mass above. With clear skies and no winds, heavy fog is virtually guaranteed. Finally, the morning sun reveals a fantasy land where bridges are ghostly apparitions and the world ends just a few feet past my wingtip.*

FOREWORD

IT IS SAID THAT EVERYONE HAS A RIVER RUNNING THROUGH THEIR HEARTS AND IMAGINATION. The Grand River has just such a presence for the one million people who reside along southern Ontario's largest inland river system.

A watershed of rare beauty and importance, the Grand has achieved coveted Canadian Heritage River status. A wild river along much of its course, the Grand and its tributaries (the Speed, Eramosa, Conestogo and Nith Rivers) link fascinating and fragile ecosystems, rare to Canada.

For most communities, the Grand was their very reason for existence. In pioneer times, fledging mills lined the river's banks, and used its abundant energy in an age before steam and electric power freed industry from the chains of riverside locations. Villages were founded around these mill sites, and from these early settlements grew our modern day cities and towns.

This process of settlement is not unique in Ontario. What makes a difference is the Grand's continued impact on the daily lives of its residents, urban and rural alike, who rely on the river and its groundwater resources for their domestic water supply. The Grand therefore has not only shaped its region's past — it will have a major role in shaping its future.

By the 1980s, individual citizens and interested groups began to recognize the Grand as a cherished natural asset and tremendous recreation resource. Much has been accomplished in the intervening decades. Almost every community is realizing the value of the river's trails, fishing and canoeing opportunities in providing a key component for enhanced quality of life and the generation of welcome tourism dollars.

CAMBRIDGE — *Natural and farm landscapes readily catch my eye. Least compelling are places where we have worked intensely to reshape forests and fields for our benefit. Little poetry is found in parking lots, factory rooftops, and stamped-out-of-the-mould subdivisions. Strangely though, these two worlds meet in a decidedly acceptable way in a golf course. I know that virtually every tree line, sand trap and pond is a re-creation of what once was. Yet the proliferation of green and spaciousness leave me with a sense of ease and comfort.*

Special note should be made however, that the Grand has proven to be more than an economic boon and recreational asset. For many, the river has leant its inspiration to art, music and literature, thus further solidifying the river's lofty status in the consciousness of its residents.

With "*The Grand River — An Aerial Journey*", aviator, author and photographer Carl Hiebert provides us with a view of the river that cannot be found behind the wheel of a car, or even from the adventurous perspective of a canoe or river-side hiking trail. As the publisher of this volume, the Grand River Conservation Foundation offers to watershed residents and visitors the unique opportunity to share this wonderful perspective, and to see the river's beauty in a new and fascinating light.

Continuing in the tradition of "*Grand River Reflections*", the Foundation's first publishing venture, proceeds from the sale of "*The Grand River — An Aerial Journey*" will be used to further the Foundation's work of supporting tangible and worthwhile local environmental enhancement projects.

As such, I hope that your enjoyment of this book will lead to your own personal flights of discovery about this Grand River of ours that is so loved by all who have come to know it.

The Honourable Lincoln M. Alexander, PC, CC, Ont QC

April, 2003

ONONDAGA — *To fly and photograph is to be in the moment. Yet sometimes the focus is broken — as prompted here by this surreal light — and curiosity pulls me into the river's past. How violent were these waters 12,000 years ago when they were first birthed by the retreating glaciers? What a curious sight it must have been to see elephant-like mammoths lumbering along these shorelines. What did the first European explorers, Brébeuf and Galinee, talk about when they discovered this pristine place and named it "La Grande"? If I could only fly back in time...*

Photographer's Notes

So what exactly are you looking for?", my friend asks as we slice through the butter-smooth sunrise air. From 500 feet, a continuous and surprising combination of angular fence lines, irregular wood lots, yellow and green fields, roll toward us in the finest of tapestries.

"I really don't know," is my honest reply, "but I'll know when I see it." She gives me a sideways glance that implies more than a hint of doubt. How can I be up here photographing for a book when I have no idea of what I want to shoot?

That's it, I realize. This is never a predictable process. And it's precisely this unknown and variability that makes flying such a seductive activity, even after 22 years.

It also brings to mind a common question asked during media interviews: "What do you think about when you're flying?" The answer has always been easy. "As little as possible."

What I have come to realize is that the most compelling images are most often the spontaneous ones. On occasion I've set out on a flight with a specific intent, for example to photograph the long shadows of trees and farm buildings in that last half hour before sunset. I might be lucky enough to bring home a few acceptable images. But I run the risk of seeing little else. Focusing on the specific almost always precludes seeing the whole.

My most rewarding and satisfying shooting occurs when there are no expectations, the mind virtually in a free-wheel mode. That's when serendipity hands me those exceptional images. It seems the subconscious is much more imaginative and spontaneous than the act of intention.

As I weave over the land, a flash of texture or colour grabs my attention. In the moment, I would be hard pressed to explain why this given scene attracts me, but it clearly does, and I don't question it. Only later, with the photograph in hand and the luxury of time, can I begin to dissect the elements that caught my eye. (*See page 87*). Would gifts be nearly as enticing if they were not initially wrapped, concealing their surprise?

Photographing for this book has been a great opportunity to stretch my wings and discover new territory. In years of flying from my friend's farm west of Elmira, I repeatedly explored Waterloo Region on my usual one-hour flights and I had come to know my back yard intimately. Farms were recognized by the layout of their buildings, my position pinpointed by a curve in a gravel road.

This is a much bigger challenge and I have to acquaint myself with unfamiliar names like Riverview, Grand Valley, Ohsweken and Dunnville. New refueling stops must be found and I began imagining greasing my wheels on grass runways that are now only circles on my map. With crisp maps, ruler, GPS coordinates and a "wish list" of photographs, I feel like a student on the first day of class, wondering what the year will bring. I relish the challenge.

CONESTOGO

To probe the southern half of the river, a grass runway at York, located approximately half way between Brantford and Lake Erie, becomes my home for a week. As happens often in aerial photography, my visit here is not nearly so much about being productive as it is learning about patience. With the exception of just one brilliantly clear Monday morning, the rest of the days are spent frustrated, staring at overcast skies and winds more suited for my acrobatic kites than my ultralight. I should have remembered — it has always been this way. In the three summer months in 1993, when I flew and photographed the eastern half of Canada for my book "*Gift of Wings*," only one day in six was suitable for my work.

But on those exceptional days, usually the first or second morning following the passage of a cold front, the magic is still here. It's the clean, razor-sharp morning light and minimal winds that invite me back into the skies with the exuberance of skipping a grade 11 algebra class.

LINWOOD

I fly low, my height often measured in but a few hundreds of feet, not thousands. (Pilots universally continue to use traditional Imperial measurements. The standardization is there for reasons of obvious safety). Whereas most aerial photographs are taken at a thousand feet or higher, this feels more like being on top of a high step ladder. Mine is a privileged, intimate view of the land.

Cruising lazily at 50 mph, I can easily identify a specific building (*see Ruthven, page 49*) or the detailed art of pattern and design *(see page 80)*. It's effortless to wind through seven rolls of film — over 200 photographs — in a two hour flight. If a scene is particularly compelling, and I have a strong sense it will qualify as a final edit for my book, I have no difficulty shooting a dozen or more pictures.

Because of relative motion — the camera is continually moving — there is a high reject ratio in taking aerial photos. To find just one absolute "keeper," a shot virtually guaranteed to qualify for the book, leaves a great smile on my face. Over half of my images are thrown out regularly. Friends are astonished to see how quickly my waste basket becomes filled with hundreds of discarded slides.

During my flights, I often reflect on my great fortune to fly and photograph this way. Ultralights are readily accessible and affordable flying machines, and have only been part of aviation in the last 25 years. (A used, single-seat ultralight can still be purchased for as little as $5,000, less than a second-hand car.) The combination of slow flight speeds and open cockpit is ideal for taking aerial photos.

BAMBERG — *If these walls could only talk, what stories would they tell? Matilda Haid knows several, for this is where she spent her childhood. The resilient walls seem metaphorically appropriate for a time when farm life was hard, but honest and good. Sadly, two separate arson fires destroyed this 1850s-built house, barn and outdoor oven, located on the right. Time and again, I never tire of rediscovering this well-hidden castle.*

During the spring and summer of 2002, when the majority of these pictures are taken, the river becomes more than a series of specific images and places. It flows to a deeper, more reflective place, and becomes a metaphor for my own journey through life.

I sense that for the first time on an early morning flight to probe the very source of the Grand. The line on my map shrinks to its smallest possible width as it traces the river north past the town of Dundalk. I have to pay sharp attention here or I'll easily lose its course. Even at an altitude of only 200 feet, the two-foot-wide stream regularly disappears beneath the undergrowth. I hang on to my precarious connection as long as I'm able, sometimes carving several circles overhead before I call out another "gotcha," in our game of hide and seek.

But predictably, the river wins. The image on page 119 is the last time I can positively identify this waterway. With a quiet decisiveness, the water splits and the two even smaller streams vanish quickly into a small woods. I criss-cross over the trees several times, hanging on to a faint hope I might pick up the trail once more. It is not to be.

After several minutes, I turn back and retrace my path southward, and begin a flight of discovery. For I now see the river not as disappearing, but as emerging. From an unknown place in these woods, two trickling streams flow out of their shaded birth sites, wind curiously across the woven grass and merge into the beginnings of a new river. In just seven days, these same waters will ultimately spill into Lake Erie.

Along the way, the river's course is various, exploring any direction except a straight line. It swells, uniting with other tributaries; stops momentarily and languishes as a lake; cascades in delight over a dam; and flows slow and insolent during its final stretch. Each bend in its passage leads to an unknown, as my own life flows with equal twists and turns, emerging from the miracle of conception to the mystery of death. My flight continues and from my privileged vantage point, I watch the unfolding of an entire life's journey.

In the captions that follow, photograph locations are defined relative to the nearest community and the Imperial measuring system is used following the standard for aviation.

WINTERBOURNE — I'm not a morning person and a jarring 5:30 a.m. alarm is the last thing I want to hear. It feels like the middle of the night. What finally motivates me to the shower and the 15 minute drive to the hanger is the anticipation of welcoming a sunrise at 200 feet (60 m). It seems the wheels only just leave the ground and I am taken instantly into another world, an ethereal place where light, ground fog and shadows weave a visual euphoria. The moment is timeless and I wish it would go on forever.

GRAND VALLEY

BADEN

GRAND VALLEY AND BADEN — I criss-crossed the Grand River watershed numerous times and anticipated the discovery of several hundred bridges. My astonishment came from the variety of sizes and styles. Numerous bowstring arch bridges have survived, ranging from single spans on the narrower upper Grand to the spectacular nine-span bridge in Caledonia (*page 30*). But surely the most innovative bridge was built by a local snowmobile club, allowing their machines to easily cross Bamberg Creek. Its construction might seem minimalist but it has the integrity to withstand spring floods, which typically sweep over the railings.

LUTHER MARSH — On occasion, locals jokingly call it "a mosquito infested frost-pocket." (The high elevation generates about the same number of cold days as Ottawa.) But for thousands of migratory birds, the dead falls, water lilies and somewhat isolated location of Luther Marsh make it a prime migration stop. Some stay longer. Several ospreys and an estimated 250 great blue herons call this home during the summer months. Conservationists lend a helping hand by replacing the fallen tress with poles stuck in the marsh bottom and building nest platforms on top.

LUTHER MARSH — Our relationship with the natural environment has often been left wanting. With the spread of farming to the upper reaches of the Grand, deforestation and wetland drainage destroyed most of the natural water retention. By the early 1930s it was not uncommon for the Grand, north of Belwood Lake, to dry completely by summer's end. Only with the creation of Luther Marsh, a 3,500-acre man-made reservoir, were seasonal flows restored.

BURFORD — The American Sweet Chestnut was once the delight of settlers who used it for everything from interior trim, to furniture, to railway ties. That ended with a devastating blight in the 1930s. But nature is amazingly resilient and at least five original Ontario trees survived, hidden deep in a Burford woodlot. They have been carefully guarded and the Burford Tree Nursery now ships out upwards of 3,000 new seedlings each year, a huge contribution toward the successful restoration of this species.

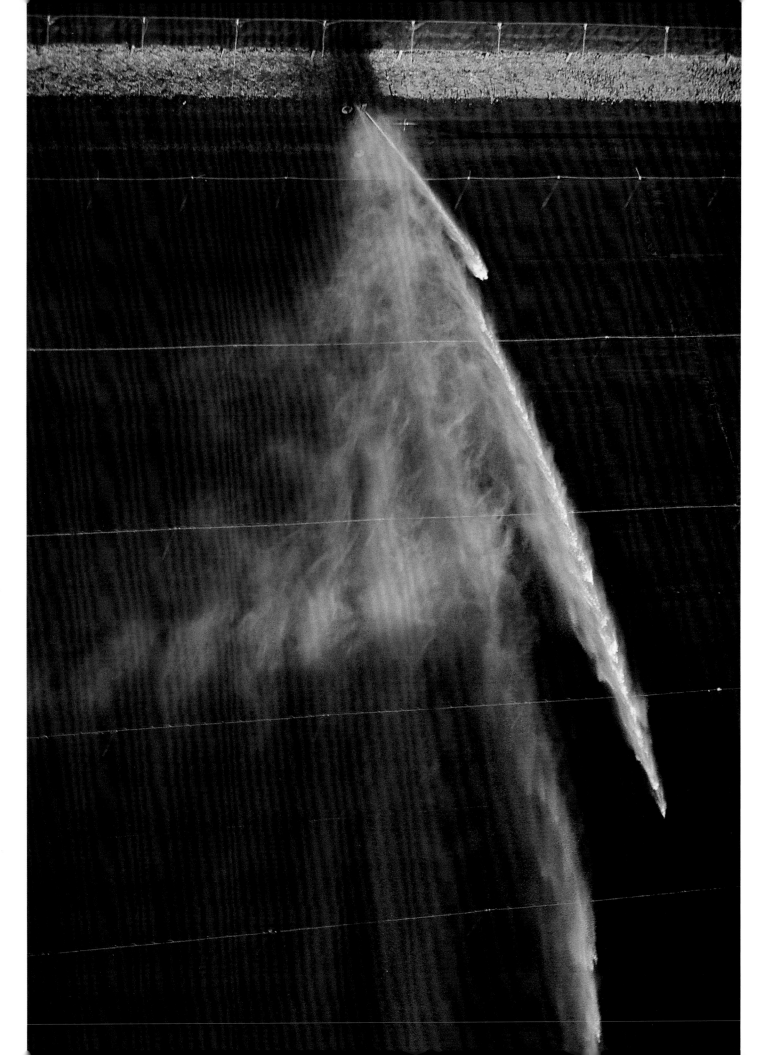

BURFORD — In a year of photographing the Grand River watershed, this picture was unquestionably the most technically difficult. We see rainbows when sunlight is spread out into its spectrum of colours and reflected back to us by water droplets, at an angle of 42 degrees or less, depending on the colour. As I wheeled above a ginseng field being irrigated, a rainbow flashed through the waterjets like a magician's sleight of hand. Did I really see it? On subsequent passes, I approached with my camera ready, but even after a dozen clicks, still was not convinced I had captured this elusive burst of colour.

INVERHAUGH — More than one-quarter million people in the larger municipalities along the Grand rely on its water for drinking. Treated effluent from over a half million people pours back into the same waterway. It's an on-going and monumental juggling act to accommodate both processes. Thanks largely to minimum flow rates and greatly improved treatment techniques, water quality has improved dramatically from 40 years ago. Through the hard work of many partners, our drinking water is considered among the safest in Ontario.

ELORA — What motivates an otherwise rational adult to spend several years and up to $40,000 dollars fixing up a 50-year-old car? Often, the reasons are sentimental and nostalgic. They want to find the same kind of car dad used to drive or perhaps have a second childhood. And of course there's always the camaraderie that comes when 250 like-minded people gather at the annual antique car show held next to the Grand River in Elora's Bissell Park.

FLORADALE — By the mid-1980s, windsurfing was the hot summer sport, with regattas held everywhere. It was novel, affordable and challenging. Then the demise. People became frustrated, waiting days for the right winds. They could golf or play tennis almost anytime. Board prices soared to more than what a used small sailboat would cost. On a breezy Saturday evening, this lone windsurfer on the Woolwich Reservoir somehow seemed emblematic for a sport that has largely come and gone.

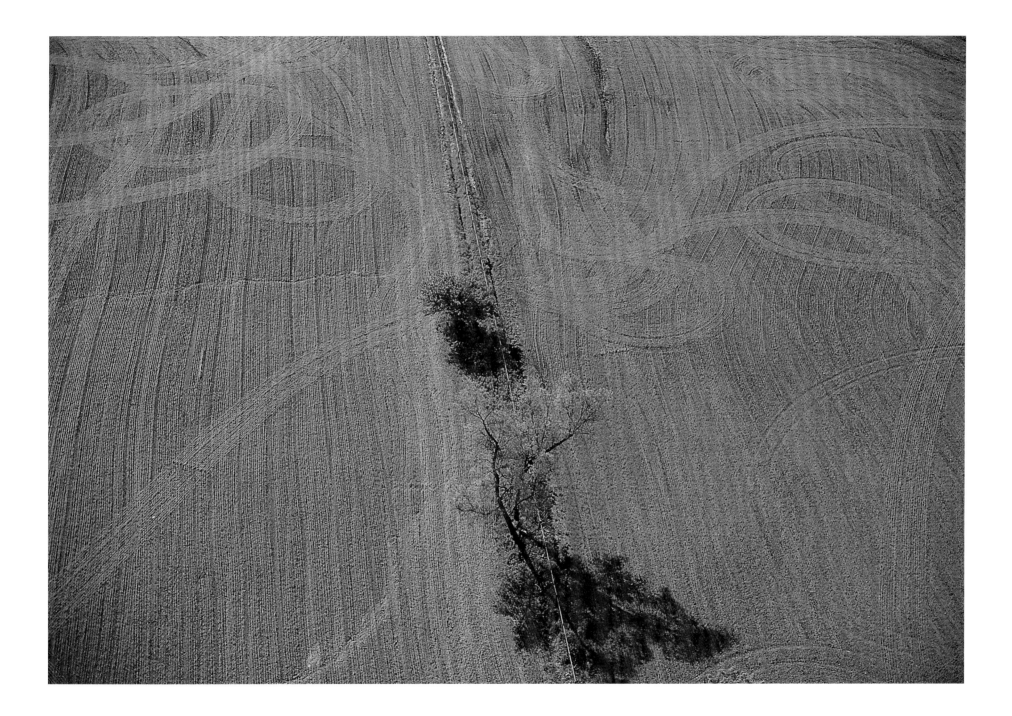

DORKING — A question often comes to mind during my flights. "Do the farmers, gardeners, and landscapers below have any idea of the art they have created?" Was this for my benefit only? The design could never be appreciated at ground level. For whatever curious reason, this farmer during spring planting has deliberately over-seeded (planted twice over) on both sides of the fence line. A possible explanation — he was emptying the remaining seed in his drill.

CALEDONIA — There's rhythmic poetry in the Caledonia bridge with its nine bowstring arches connecting two sides of town. Just as important, it connects the spirits of local residents who take great pride in the bridge's historic status. Bedecked with Canadian banners, it is the town's unquestionable landmark. But they wonder about its future. After 75 years it has tired under ever-increasing traffic and at this writing, discussions continue as to whether it should be carefully repaired or simply replaced.

YATTON — There are buried secrets only the farmer can explain. What are the green lines cutting diagonally through his fields of hay, corn and wheat? They are drainage tiles, buried about three feet (one metre) deep, to rid the land of excess water. Three factors explain the telltale lines. The land dries quickest here in spring, forcing roots to grow deeper for moisture, ultimately producing a healthier, greener plant. Secondly, plant roots located between the drainage tiles are often supersaturated after a heavy rain, a detriment to growth. Lastly, the downward flow of water creates vertical cavities in the soil, which aerate the land and stimulate growth.

WASHINGTON — Long before the invention of the electric refrigerator, early pioneers packed their precious foodstuffs in cakes of ice, and covered all with a pile of sawdust to slow the melting process. A similar construction formed what are today called "kettle lakes." When the glaciers retreated from this area 12,000 years ago, large blocks of ice were randomly buried under insulating layers of sand and gravel. Because the climate was much more severe than today, it took up to 3,000 years for the ice to melt, resulting in the depressions still visible in farm fields today.

CAMBRIDGE — The Whistle Bear golf course is a lesson in transformation, from an exhausted gravel pit to a true Championship design. Defined as a "links" course, in that there are intentionally no trees, the long 7,400 yards of fairways are particularly distinctive from the air. The proliferation of 103 sand traps and fescue (areas of long brown grass, which are never watered) are insidious in their ability to make golf balls disappear. Actor Dennis Quaid played here in the summer of 2002 and said, "I must have left behind 12 sleeves (36 balls) in your fescue." For many, golf will always remain an exercise in humility.

YATTON — On an early morning flight, I imagine this to be a place of continuity, of multi-generational farms. But should I fly lower, much lower, and could read the mailbox names, I would learn of a more complex community. Visser, Martin, Kramer and Schill: Dutch, Old Order Mennonite, Markam Mennonite and Catholic. Like their city counterparts, but at a slower rate, these population groups are constantly shifting and re-defining their places. Yet they are also held together by their work — the fields of corn, soybeans, wheat and hay, the barns of beef, cows and poultry.

ELMIRA — It took 35 years to mature from a simple idea, but in 2000 the Elmira Maple Syrup Festival marched into the Guinness Book of World Records. Eighty thousand people, on that Saturday morning in April, drenched their golden-brown pancakes with the freshest of maple syrup — 600 gallons (2700 litres) of it — and enjoyed what has become one of the region's great family events. Equally impressive is that over the years, the festival has raised more than $1 million for various charities.

KITCHENER — It's the central pipeline of Canada's economy and it's never big enough. On an average day, more than 100,000 vehicles zip down Highway 401 past the Cambridge area. With growth in Waterloo Region consistently high, and more and more freight being shipped by trucks, it's increasingly rare to find a relaxing stretch of empty highway. Additional lanes cost in excess of $2 million per kilometre so motorists can realistically expect to sing the traffic blues for years to come.

CONESTOGO — The farmer is a pragmatic man taking pride in straight rows, no weeds and healthy crops. That much I understand. But what inspired this creative twist? It puzzles me as much today, even after speaking to numerous farmers, searching for an explanation. Perhaps a friend said it best, "It's just the heartbeat of the land."

LISBON — "St. Jacobs Country" visitors are invariably drawn to the "horse and buggy Mennonites," but the label is not that simple. Two larger conservative Mennonite groups dominate the gently rolling countryside - the Old Order and Dave Martin Mennonites. Not so commonly known is the Amish community which reaches west from Linwood and north from Stratford. Only a closer look reveals some of their differences — open buggies, bearded married men and buttonfree coats. Like their Mennonite counterparts, the Amish live close to the land where church and community mean everything.

WATERLOO — They were humble beginnings. Thirty years ago a few hopeful farmers and merchants set up stands beside a local livestock auction. Today, the St. Jacobs Farmers' Market is one of the most popular and authentic farmers' markets in all of Canada. On a summer Saturday the market attracts upwards of 20,000 people. Six hundred vendors fill aisle after aisle with everything from summer sausage and maple syrup produced locally by Old Order Mennonites, to fresh fruits and vegetables from across Ontario.

WATERLOO — When a handful of University of Waterloo students first organized a small Canada Day celebration at Columbia Lake 20 years ago, they could not have imagined its future. For upwards of 50,000 Kitchener-Waterloo residents, it's an annual summer ritual. But the afternoon of games, music, food and face painting is largely a precursor to 20 minutes of nighttime fantasy. With Columbia Lake reflecting back the magic, fireworks tear apart the skies and in the moment, allow everyone to be a child again.

KITCHENER & WATERLOO

KITCHENER, WATERLOO & CAMBRIDGE — My favourite place to float through the skies is at a height of just a few hundred feet. There's more detail and greater clarity. But when a passing cold front cleared the skies I called a friend and we climbed in his Cessna to 5,000 feet (1500 m). The visibility was breath-taking, well over 50 miles (75 km). For orientation, the Kitchener and Waterloo photo (above), looks north. Deer Ridge golf course is on the lower left and Highway 8 is on the right, running diagonally to intersect with the Conestoga Parkway. The Cambridge view (opposite), looks southeast, with the Galt golf course in the foreground and Highway 8, stretching toward Hamilton, on the top left.

CAMBRIDGE

CONESTOGO LAKE — Nature's default mode is diversity and randomness. Then why would any forester execute such an intentional design? Ironically, it was an innovative experiment to foster the co-development of conifers and hardwoods. Previous reforestation attempts, where maple and ash trees where planted randomly with neighbouring red and white pines, resulted in a high attrition rate for the hardwoods. Forty years after these trees were planted, this vertical view clearly speaks to a successful experiment.

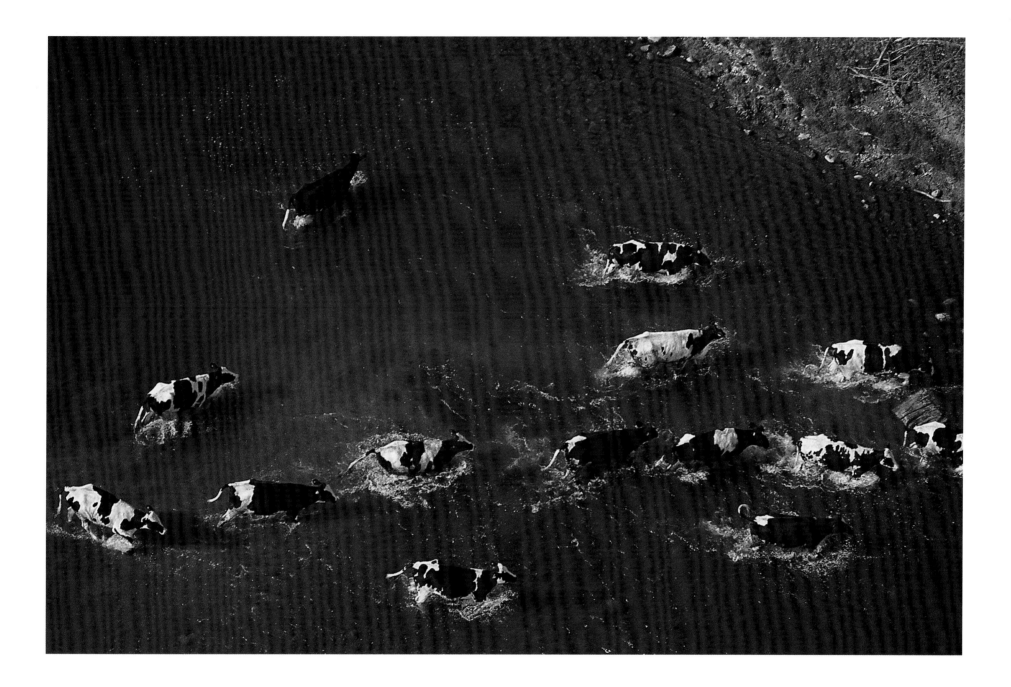

GLEN ALLAN — They made me laugh. As if suddenly possessed, the cows charged en masse across the Conestogo River. Where was Moses to wave his rod and guarantee a dry passage? This exodus happens rarely these days as the GRCA, through a fencing and tree planting program, educates and compensates farmers to protect streams and rivers. The results are dramatic. A farmer spoke of how his dad enjoyed fishing until one day the fish went away. Today, his grandchildren can once again snag a trout or two in the same old fishing holes.

GUELPH — Aggregates are typically extracted in one of two ways — by digging a quarry into bedrock or, as shown here, by mining a glacial deposit. These deposits were formed when large amounts of water carrying gravel gushed out of melting glaciers approximately 12,000 years ago. This particular colour results from a concentration of suspended clay particulates which scatter light more in the shorter wavelengths of the visible spectrum — the same phenomenon which, on a finer level, makes the sky blue.

ELMIRA — We drink, shower, flush and do laundry with such familiarity there's little reason to wonder how the water got there. I wouldn't have expected the estimated 50 elevated water storage facilities in the Grand River watershed. Water is pumped into these tanks and natural gravitational force ensures a continuous supply to our homes, factories and fire hydrants, even when electricity is off. At 1.5 million gallons (approximately 7 million litres), the Elmira tower holds enough fresh water to supply the town for just two days.

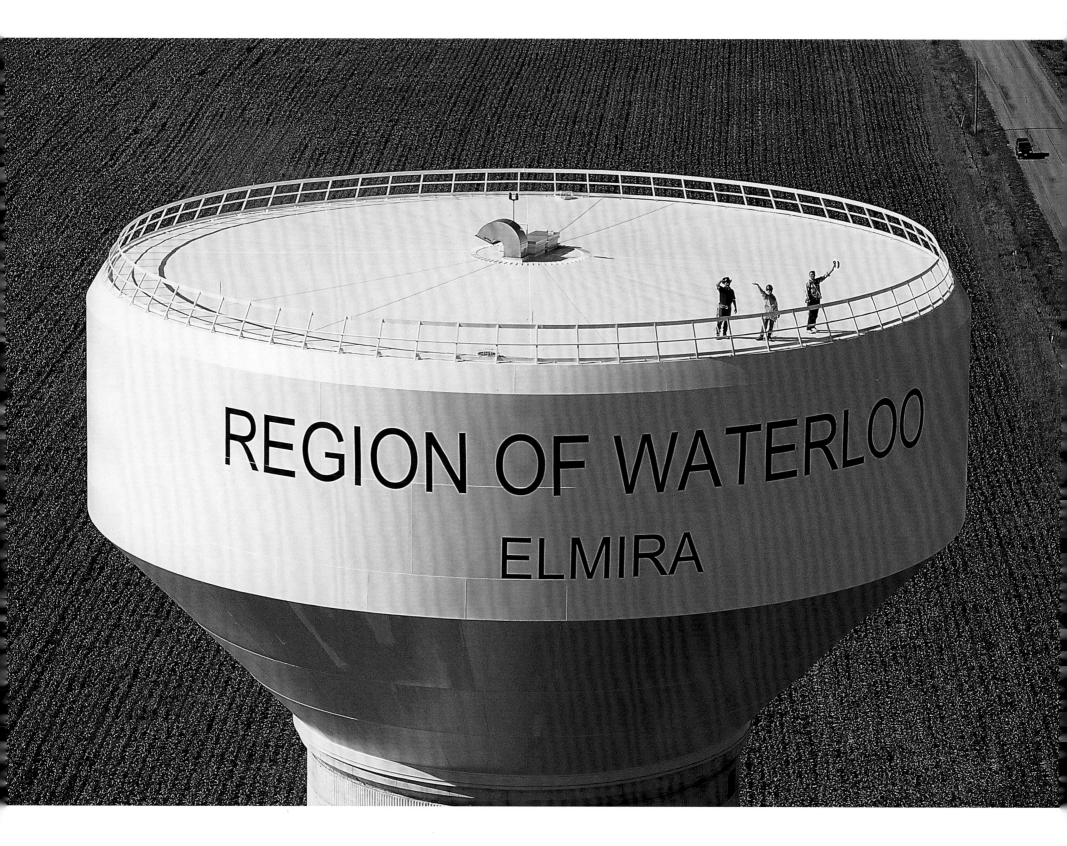

MARYHILL — "Sierra Delta X-Ray, report Maryhill." It's not often that pilots are first directed to a church while looking for a runway. It so happens the St. Boniface Church marks the northern boundary of the Waterloo Regional Airport control zone. The distinctive church tower, built on the highest local hill, makes it an easily recognized landmark from as far as 10 miles (15 km) away. To see it finally emerge through poor visibility is perhaps as comforting for weary, home-bound pilots as for souls searching for solace inside.

CAYUGA — When Scottish industrialist and entrepreneur David Thompson built his dream house known as Ruthven in 1845, the local, mostly Irish residents were not long in calling it "Thompson's Folly." For an immigrant worker living in a one-room log cabin, this three storey, 36-room house, must have seemed outrageous in both size and style. Fortunately, the house survived both the skeptics and the years, and stands today as a rare example of Classical Greek Revival architecture. Particularly captivating is the central oval spiral staircase that winds through all three floors and ends at the huge skylight. I felt privileged to view that same window from a perspective Mr. Thompson, for all his wealth, could have never imagined.

PARIS — Swallows fly to Capistrano and bicyclists have to race. Nearly 1,000 riders charged through the starting line in the ninth annual Paris to Ancaster race in April, 2002. Part of the lure lies in the unknown. One year the weather changed from sunny skies to thunderstorms and then to ankle deep snow, with riders struggling the entire 45 miles (75 km). They arrived exhausted and expected little in terms of trophies or recognition. But each year they return. The friendly rivalry, thrill of the unknown, and testing of physical limits is motivation enough.

KITCHENER — The Region of Waterloo is one of Canada's fastest growing communities, averaging about 7,000 new residents annually. Newcomers are attracted by numerous factors — quality of life, a diversified economy including a burgeoning high-tech sector, wide range of housing, good infrastructure and close proximity to Toronto. While traditional subdivisions remain popular, there's growing interest in inner-city living. With municipal boundaries firmly established, limiting urban expansion, regional planners are challenged to manage growth for the benefit of all.

CONESTOGO — October. For aerial photography, this should be the year's visual highlight. All summer, production of green chlorophyll has masked the true colours hidden in these leaves. Shortened days and cooler temperatures finally slow the process, allowing the oaks, maples, birches and poplars to present their annual exhibition. But the flamboyance may not be as spectacular in times of drought, as repeated dry summers take their toll. The trees are stressed and many leaves turn brown prematurely. They fall earthbound, scarcely touched by nature's colourful brush.

NEWTON — Ernest and Nelly Hofer have always lived outside the box. A regimented Swiss farming community was much too confining for their free-wheeling spirits so they packed their trunks for Canada. Fifteen years later they celebrated that decision, and 20 years of a wonderful marriage, by creating a 50 acre (20 hectare) corn maze — likely the world's largest. During the summer of 2001, more than 6,000 people turned left, right, scratched their heads, and wondered if they would remain lost in Ontario forever.

DORKING — Who was this man? Whatever inspired him to cultivate such an outrageous pattern? As a farm boy I'd spent days on a tractor, but found this baffling in the extreme. I had to know, and later that day drove back to visit. It seemed obvious to the farmer. By crossing over diagonally at the end of each section, he not only efficiently cultivated his field twice over, but also leveled the rough furrows from last autumn's ploughing.

BELWOOD LAKE

BELWOOD LAKE AND GUELPH LAKE — The creation of three lakes in the Grand River watershed — Belwood, Guelph and Conestogo — proved a huge recreational boon. In addition to accommodating thousands of boaters, anglers and cottagers, the lakes are scheduled months in advance for water sport events, festivals and gatherings. Guelph Lake, with no cottages and a spacious campground, is particularly suited for hosting large-scale events. It was stretched to capacity in 1985 when 25,000 Boys Scouts, from every Canadian province, literally covered the grounds with over 5,000 tents.

GUELPH LAKE

ROCKWOOD — Like mills everywhere, the Harris Woolen Mill in Rockwood was born of the river and became a victim of modern technology. The serene setting, with the Eramosa River and its unique potholes, was dramatically altered when a Halloween night fire left behind only a burned-out shell. Yet a grandeur remains and uninformed visitors often wonder "What castle was this?" Theatrical plays, TV commercials, music videos and weddings have all used the mill as a dramatic backdrop.

GUELPH — John Galt was a visionary. He established the town of Guelph in 1827 with the dream that it would become the center of commerce for all of southwestern Ontario. His friend Bishop Macdonell concurred and constructed the foundation for a church six times larger than the present one. A reality check — a quick tally of anticipated costs — resulted in a more modest cathedral. Even so, the Church of Our Lady remains a classical Guelph landmark and perhaps the most exquisitely beautiful Catholic church in all of North America.

GUELPH — If islands floated like ships, Guelph Lake Island would surely sink under the weight of 5,000 campers and music lovers. The annual family event has earned the reputation as one of the best in Ontario, attracting world-class talent including Bruce Cockburn, Bare Naked Ladies and Laura Smith. For three days, rain or shine, guitars, drums, and fiddles reverberate across the lake. What do the resident seagulls and geese make of this strange musical intrusion into their world? There's also little sleep for the 1,000 or so volunteers who camp out near the performance tents.

LINWOOD — "It's springtime of the year, and that sure puts a feller in gear." For a Dave Martin Mennonite farmer, cultivating with four Belgian horses on a new field just about defines a perfect spring day. The quietness and closeness to the land could never be found on a tractor. These two teams — neighbours commonly work together — will cultivate their 10 acre (4 hectare) field in about four hours. The Mennonites not only consider this a less costly way of farming (a good workhorse costs about $2,000), but reflects their commitment of hanging on to at least some traditions in a rapidly changing world.

CROSSHILL — They looked like medieval war machines, waiting for a command to charge, or fire, or do something quite extraordinary. They will do nothing, for this is the threshing machine graveyard, as it's known locally — most likely the only one in Canada. Forty years ago, the father of C. and M. Bauman identified an opportunity to collect worn-out and abandoned machines and recycle them for parts or scrap metal. It's part-time work to supplement their farming income and over the years they've processed more than 1,000 machines.

AYR — Things are not always as they appear. Starting in the 1980s, dozens of rural railway branchlines were removed from smaller communities. Had Canadian rail transportation reached the end of its tracks? In fact, today the main railway corridors carry more freight tonnage than ever. This "Galt Sub" line of the CPR through Ayr easily carries 25 trains a day, many with upwards of 100 cars. Only the people have gone elsewhere. With the ease and affordability of flight, many Canadians will never know the nostalgic, rhythmic click clack, click clack, of wheels on a ribbon of steel.

WEST MONTROSE — Local resident George Jupp has always been fascinated with the Covered Bridge. But he thought he was seeing it for the last time about 50 years ago. While flying overhead, his sightseeing passenger suddenly panicked and jammed the control stick forward, sending them both toward a certain spiraling death. George yelled, tried to free the controls and finally — precisely as he'd been taught in ground school — whacked his passenger unconscious with a fire extinguisher. He hasn't seen his passenger since. George is now better known for a scale model he has constructed of this well-known bridge.

ELMIRA — Farmers are known for their resourcefulness. When area farmer and ultralight pilot Perry Weber asked his girlfriend Karen to go flying with him one Saturday morning, he hoped to launch an even more daring question. She said yes.

BRESLAU — Pilots at Waterloo Regional Airport, accustomed to radio commands and never-ending procedures, might find an earlier era of flight hard to imagine. When this airport opened in 1950, there were no taxiways or control tower. Cloth-covered Piper Cubs and Fleet Canucks passed each other regularly — one taxiing down the right side of the runway, the other flashing by on landing. It was a "see and be seen" kind of flying and considered a safe thing to do. With today's corporate jets blasting down 5,000-foot (1500 m) runways, the taxiways allow controllers and pilots alike to breathe easier.

KITCHENER — Nestled on the edge of the Grand River, just before it crosses Highway 401, is one of Waterloo Region's highly recognized icons — the Pioneer Memorial Tower. The modest, Swiss-style stone tower marks the first farm settlements by the Pennsylvania German settlers in 1800–03. From its upper viewing deck, one can imagine dust drifting from the Black Walnut Trail as the pioneers slowly rolled northward in their quest for fertile land. Near the tower, a few fading gravestones have survived, the names of Betzner and Sherk pointing at our ancestral heritage.

SCOTLAND — Ginseng has been used as medical herb for more than 5,000 years, particularly in China. More recently, with reduced tobacco acreage, farmers in the Scotland–Waterford area have planted several thousand acres of this extremely labour-intensive crop. Entire fields are installed with fence posts and wire before planting, and then covered with a black cloth or wood slats for partial shading. It will take three to five years before the roots are harvested, with most of the product shipped to China. Daily users claim numerous benefits including increased energy and improved memory.

ELORA — For its small size, the village of Elora supports a large reputation. The quaint distinctiveness of its many rubble-stone buildings are appealing to tourists and movie producers alike. Several movies have been shot here, including "An American Christmas Carol" starring Henry Winkler. Slicing through the edge of town is the Elora Gorge — a timeless place with 70-foot vertical walls, pristine campsites and challenging whitewater for kayakers. More recently, the town is gaining fame as a popular artists' community, having converted the old village school to an arts centre with galleries and resident artists.

ELORA — Before the proliferation of community and back-yard pools, 'the old swimming hole' was the place to be on a hot July weekend. The Elora Quarry is one of the few such haunts to survive. Its popularity is understandable. The location is ideal, just a half hour drive from several area cities. Spring fed water guarantees a refreshing swim. And despite all the warning signs, the ten-metre-high vertical walls still tempt youth to prove their mettle as they scream down in a body-smacking plunge.

ELORA — On an overhead flight, the first view of the Elora Research Station gives the sense of a farm gone wild. The barns are too big, too prolific, and the crops too numerous and varied. But actually, the research is broken down into hundreds of small projects — experiments in crop rotation, food safety, improved feeds, and environmental sustainability — all ultimately aimed for the good of the consumer. At 1,620 acres (650 hectares), this provincially-owned and University of Guelph-run facility is one of the largest and most important agriculture research stations in Canada.

ELMIRA — A flight from Elmira to Elora takes me directly over the North Woolwich Swamp. For an area once completely forested, this 613 acre (248 hectare), unbroken back-lot wooded swamp is now an anomaly as one of the largest intact forest tracts in Waterloo Region. Its long narrow shape originated from early settlers who typically left a bush lot at the back of their farms. The forest is of great hydrological value, being the headwater for several streams. Thanks to its protected status as an Environmentally Sensitive Area, it will remain for many years.

DAMASCUS RESERVOIR

CROSSHILL — Habitat changes following European settlement shifted the balance for the area's wildlife. Black bear and moose headed north to less disturbed homes while white-tailed deer benefited from the change. Old-growth forests offered limited food at ground level, but the clearing of trees and their replacement by acres of cultivated corn, beans and apples were ideal for the deer's propagation. Deer prefer the twilight hours and are usually skittish at my unexpected aerial arrivals. Several times, however, bucks pawed the ground, shook their antlers, and defied my low-level visit.

HAWKESVILLE — Boomer Creek flows through the heart of Mennonite farming country in Waterloo Region, a captivating landscape I judge to be one of the most beautiful in the world. These are still family farms, usually 100 acres (40 hectares) in size, which survive by their diversity. To see a team of burly Clydesdales carve a black furrow, or a field of gold-rich wheat transformed to patterned rows of sheaves, is a visual cornucopia, a view I will never tire of, the reason I fly.

HAWKESVILLE

SPEEDSIDE

HAWKESVILLE AND SPEEDSIDE — It happens each summer. At the end of July and into early August, the farmers offer their unknowing gifts to those of us who wing overhead. It's a year's worth of work, a limited showing of their best pieces. The gallery changes annually, with new combinations of colour, texture and design as the crops are rotated. For all the farmer's effort, few people are privileged to have this aerial gallery tour. I often wish there was opportunity to land and offer my empty seat to these earth-bound artist-farmers.

LINWOOD — It is an inspired tapestry, rich layers twisted in an almost hypnotic design. This wheat field pattern is known as "lodging." Just prior to reaching maturity, grain stalks are barely strong enough to support their heads. Wind and lashing rain from a summer storm can flatten a field in minutes. It's a disappointment for the farmer to watch part of his anticipated harvest slip beneath the blades and go to waste behind his combine or grain binder.

WINTERBOURNE — Peter Tillich's nursery has a severe case of the blues, but it took Peter 16 patient years to accomplish that. The seed stock of his Colorado Blue Spruce is possibly the only one in the world that consistently produces blue trees. As a result, his ornamental trees are in demand from Quebec to Oregon. The bluish colour emanates from a natural coating on each needle. Harsh winter winds tend to fade the intensity but each spring, new growth restores the cherished colour.

WALLENSTEIN — In our consumer-oriented society, more is said to be better. Pilots buy turbocharged engines, polish their wings and fly higher and faster in pursuit of an elusive goal. There is another way. A few, like retired fighter pilot Tom Jeary, have learned that the enjoyment of the countryside is inversely proportional to the speed you fly over it. What could come closer to the perfect birds'-eye view than floating through the sky in a padded leather chair while suspended under a parachute canopy?

ST. JACOBS — How often can I fly over the same countryside and still be surprised by new images? Never, in 20 years, have I seen spring bursting with such exuberance. In the middle of a dandelion-swept field, a solitary oak stretches its bare limbs to the spring sky. Leaves of delicate green unfold with the lengthening days and another cycle of the seasons begins.

PORT MAITLAND — Just east of where the Grand River spills into Lake Erie, the Mohawk Island Lighthouse still marks a safe harbour. Lacking nothing in its 1848 construction, its four-foot-thick (1.3 m) walls have largely survived the years of pounding waves and winds. Seeing it from above reminded me of the metaphorical wisdom I once learned from a friend: "To be a good lighthouse, you don't have to wander all over the island looking for ships to save. You just have to stand there and shine."

GLEN MORRIS — It often happens that a scene snags my attention, yet in the moment of photographing I don't know why. The anomaly of a singular grain field was obviously eye-catching, but there was more. A certain tension resided between the field's sharp angles and the soothing lines of the lazy river. Even more intriguing was an implied exclusivity. Thanks to the dividing hill and thick row of trees, neither farmer nor river canoeist would have any sense of each other's presence. That larger, privileged view was mine alone.

FERGUS — Numerous superlatives describe the Fergus Scottish Festival and Highland Games — world's largest highland dancing event (900 dancers), biggest gathering of clans (45), and some of the best stories. In 1972, the parade ground was already packed with pipers when Premier William Davis arrived belatedly in his helicopter for the grand opening. People shoved aside to clear a small landing area when downwash from the rotor blades sent hundreds of kilts flapping past their owners' ears. Old-timers say a dreadful moan was heard. Was it the bagpipes, inadvertently squeezed, or the crowd, seeing an age-old secret revealed?

ELORA — Each year, every Ontario resident uses the equivalent of one tandem dump truck of gravel. Aggregate is used in everything from an abrasive in toothpaste, concrete for high rises, and asphalt for highways. The Grand River watershed is abundantly rich in its gravel and sand resource, which significantly reduces the costs of providing local infrastructure. A typical pit takes 20 to 25 years to be fully mined, supplying enough gravel to build a two-lane highway from Windsor to the Quebec border.

HAWKESVILLE — This gravel pit is a just a few minutes flight from my grass runway and I've winged overhead many times, rarely giving it a second glance. I feel little connection to this broken landscape, especially in contrast with the beauty of the surrounding Mennonite farms. But on an early morning flight, I am breathless. The upward sweep from the complexity and heaviness of the stones, to the serenity of the ethereal clouds, feels surrealistic, more than I can take in.

It is so intensely charged with contrast and metaphor that I almost forget to lift my camera and capture this serendipitous moment on film.

FERGUS — It's not commonly known that Fergus is possibly the only intentionally planned settlement in Upper Canada. Adam Ferguson, an aggressive Scottish entrepreneur, convinced authorities to sell him and a partner 7,400 acres (3,000 hectares) of land encompassing Little Falls on the Grand River. The combination of water power to operate mills and rich loam soil made this area ideal. In return, he promised to create a prosperous community within two years. His prospective settlers were hand-picked friends and relatives from the home country — and well off. As a result, Fergus had more lawyers per square foot than anywhere in Canada. People skilled to work with their hands were in short supply and the practical Irish moved in to fill the gap, but for years the Scots and Irish remained largely segregated in this innovative community.

FERGUS — On a drive from Elora to Fergus it's impossible not to be wowed by the stately elegance of the Wellington County Museum and Archives building. It has lived two distinct lives. In the 1870s, numerous House of Industry and Refuge facilities were built to care for the aged, destitute and orphans. This is the oldest such building to survive and is now designated a National Historic Site. By 1971 its retirement residents had moved to a new facility and this prominent building now houses much of the county's history.

ELORA — "I've flown throughout Canada," reflects balloon pilot Dave Falla, "and there's no better place to fly than the Grand River valley. There are birds and wildlife everywhere — blue herons, red tailed hawks, and lots of deer. It's such a joy to fly with people who have never seen their own backyards from the air. They can't believe how neat and how diverse this area is. The sensation is like sitting still in your favourite chair and watching the world drift by underneath."

HESSON — Trying to photograph my own shadow is an exercise in momentary confusion. To ensure tack-sharp images at low altitudes requires panning my camera as the subject flashes by. After thousands of aerial photographs, the procedure has become automatic. This time it almost didn't work. My camera kept swinging naturally to the right, trying to keep the dandelions in focus, while the shadow leapt out of the viewfinder. I was befuddled. It took several tries to break an old habit and hold the camera steady on my companion shadow.

HAWKESVILLE — Keith Snyder has fine teenage memories of a neighbour's swimming hole. When he asked his own growing children — three boys and three girls — to choose between a new house or pond, the choice was unanimous. The result is one of the more popular places to be on a hot summer's night, with up to 50 kids making communal waves. To ensure a steady and refreshing water supply, Keith installed a windmill to pump well water into the pond. Winter skating and hockey are simply a bonus.

KINGWOOD — It's been said the ear craves the familiar, the eye the novel. We delight in listening repeatedly to our favourite CDs, yet photograph new discoveries on our vacation travels. But even within the visual world, there are consistent elements that shape the more compelling images. These solitary elm trees reflect our inherent attraction for groupings of odd, rather than even, numbers.

ST. JACOBS — The St. Jacobs story is one of radical transformation. By the mid-1970s this typical rural community, with its flour mill and grocery store closing their doors, appeared destined to become another "has been" village. To preserve the authenticity of the distinctive Mennonite heritage, businessman Milo Shantz created a new identity. Today more than one million visitors enjoy the picturesque streets, shops and rural tours each year. It seems quite natural for a horse and buggy to trot past Tim Hortons, in a place where cultures overlap with a delightful curiosity.

CONESTOGO — In over 20 years of flying in Waterloo Region, there are several "flight paths" which have become my favourites — brief, touchstone journeys which consistently delight. Heading north toward the village of Conestogo along its namesake river is one of these. The river seems lazy here, intentional in its meandering before it spills into the Grand, as though the land and water have come to an understanding of the space they need. Spring flood waters might charge across adjacent fields, often littering them with ice blocks and debris. Just days later, they retire to a gentler flow, suggesting it had always been this way, a place of harmony and timelessness.

PORT MAITLAND — A hundred years ago, this guardian community of the Grand River glowed in the tourism spotlight. Thousands of passengers steamed across the lake from Erie and Buffalo to picnic on the beaches or fish their quota of sturgeon, pike and muskie. But the party largely ended when the automobile came into widespread use. Suddenly the summer visitor could cover more miles and had wider choices. In an attempt to revive tourism, the government recently completed a major facelift of the piers and lighthouse. Perhaps the days of former glory will return again.

CONESTOGO LAKE — Boaters on Conestogo Lake are likely unaware they race above fields, foundations of farm buildings and stories of yesteryear. In 1958, a dam built for flood control and low-flow augmentation flooded 1,800 acres (730 hectares) of farmland and river valley. Mary and John Stinson weren't keen to move from the house they'd been born in, even though newly formed lake waters lapped at their front door. A neighbour rowed over to visit, knocked on the front door with a paddle and asked Mary if she wanted to tour the lake. Seeing its size must have convinced Mary things were never going to be the same. She and her brother moved shortly thereafter.

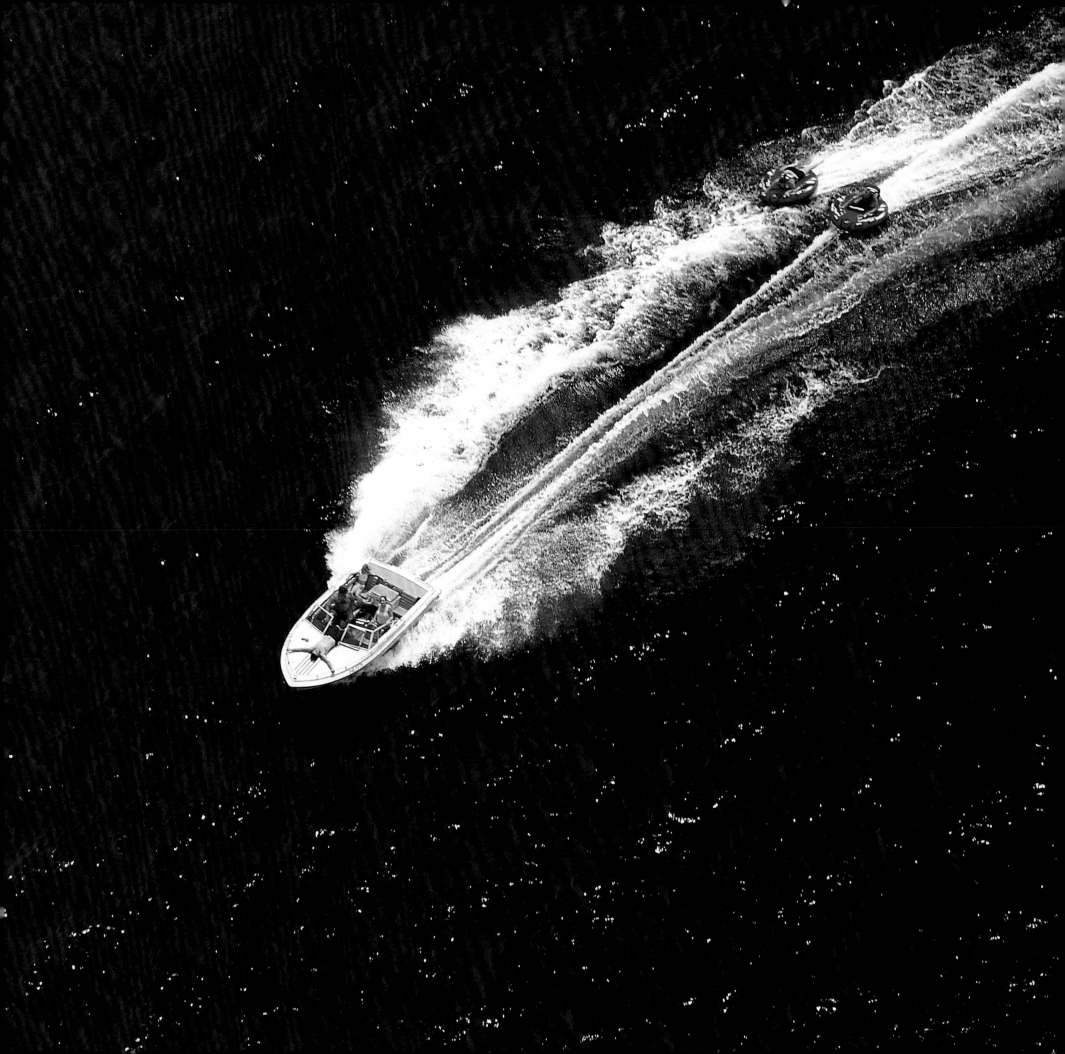

ROTHSAY — An old joke floats around farming circles. "Did you hear the Ministry of Agriculture is going to ban round bales? Too many complaints from cattle they can't get a square meal." Disgruntled cattle and bad jokes notwithstanding, round bales are advantageous. One bale is the equivalent of approximately 25 square bales, greatly reducing handling and transportation time and labour. Unfortunately, round bales roll and farmers must remain extra cautious in moving these weighty dinner snacks.

MT. PLEASANT — The image made me smile. Over a mile away the hotels of a mammoth Monopoly game sprang out of the surrounding tobacco fields. Several generations of families have methodically maintained these 70-year-old traditional tobacco kilns. Once picked, the tobacco leaves hang in the curing barns for one to two weeks before being sorted and shipped. The newly refurbished steel roofs are so prominent that local pilots flying into Brantford airport use them as a common landmark.

CONESTOGO LAKE — Light shapes everything, especially from the aerial perspective. This is the same lake that appears on the opposite page. What distinguishes these hugely different impressions is a shift of time and a slightly dissimilar vantage point. Water is particularly variable in its dance with light. A circling flight at this time of day sees the lake transition from a blinding white to a darkness almost matching the land.

NEW HAMBURG — It seems that vehicles become more efficient with time. Factory-fresh cars arrive only 10 at a time on a tractor-trailer. But only 15 to 20 years later, stripped of wheels, batteries and radiators, they are flattened and packed 30 per load for their final road trip — an ignoble end at recycling plants. Benny's Auto Parts recycles 800 or more vehicles annually. It's a rapidly changing business as the high cost of repairs means more accident vehicles than ever are scrapped and sent straight to the shredders.

DAMASCUS — The land crests slightly near the village of Monck. A five kilometre-wide rain shower here could end up in three different watersheds — the Grand, Conestogo, and Saugeen. Some of it will flow to the Damascus Reservoir, built in 1980 as a low-flow augmentation reservoir. Spring runoff water is collected and carefully metered into the Conestogo River over the dry summer months to maintain a steady flow.

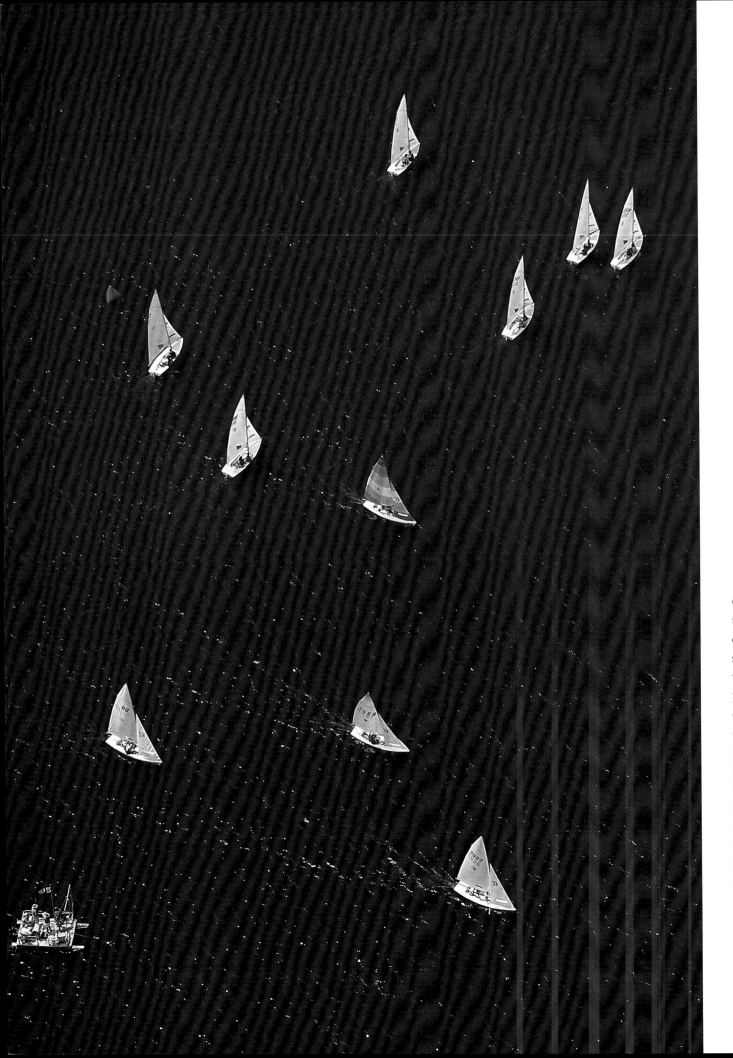

CONESTOGO LAKE — Three times in the past, the Ontario Summer Games have been played out on Conestogo Lake. The lake's relatively small size and irregular shoreline play havoc with the wind, making sailing here anything but predictable. Sometimes described as a "real life chess game," sailing is a challenging combination of athletics and tactics. To bring home the gold, the sailors must respond automatically to their procedures — hiking, trimming sails, and finding their optimal heading. Simultaneously, it's a heads-up game of outsmarting the competition — being first through the start line, knowing when to join a tack, or blanket someone's wind, as illustrated here in the top right of this photograph.

CONESTOGO LAKE — Another day of competition begins at the Ontario Summer Games rowing competition. Kitchener's Sara Niblock is keen. For months, she's been getting up at 4 a.m., five days a week, to practice on calm water. It's huge discipline for an 18-year-old. At the end of three days, she wears no medals, but is just as enthusiastic. For most participants in this peaceful sport, competition is strong but winning is secondary to the joy of effort and having a good time.

OHSWEKEN — The Six Nations Reserve near Brantford has birthed several Canadian celebrities: most famously actors Graham Greene and Jay Silverheels (Tonto), and poet E. Pauline Johnson. Particularly notable is long distance runner Tom Longboat. Despite poverty and poor training, he became one of the world's best runners, including winning the Boston Marathon in 1907. Stories still circulate of the bets won when he sprinted against racehorses. He was a Canadian hero and his achievements still inspire people who have a love of running fast.

CALEDONIA — Fred Thompson farms some curious fields — islands in the Grand River. That demands a few unusual considerations. Spring planting doesn't happen until the seasonal high waters have receded to guarantee a safe fording. Even so, when Fred's tractor once ran out of gas mid-passage, he still got his feet wet. The fields are never too dry and since 1924, when his father purchased this farm, have consistently produced good yields of hay, wheat and corn.

ALMA — To fly the length of the Grand is to sit through a fascinating lesson in geology, agriculture and economics. Receding glaciers left behind a variety of soil types as they retreated north — clay, sand plains, rich clay loams and wetlands. The basis for crop types and difficulty or ease of farming were largely set by these soil parameters. Today, less than 20 percent of the population is rural, but accounts for a disproportionately large part of our economy. The central Waterloo–Wellington area is particularly rich in dairy, beef, poultry and cash crops and was once labeled by Statistics Canada as an "Agricultural Nirvana."

BELWOOD

BELWOOD & BRANTFORD — Flight takes me into a world of surprises. Cresting a hill, or passing over a forest, gives little indication of what lies on the other side. The discoveries never end and it is this fascination that pulls me back into the skies year after year. Often, my "ah-ha" discoveries are almost exclusive to the aerial view, as illustrated here. The show-case country home was discreetly built well away from the highway while a weary barn, located miles in another direction, had largely disappeared in its return to Mother Earth.

BRANTFORD

LINWOOD — Perhaps somewhat like writing, we rarely notice the highways we travel unless they need improvement. Improper verb tenses and dangling participles can jar us as readily as potholes and narrow lanes. Replacing this deteriorating culvert was budgeted and designed more than a year in advance. It took detailed planning, a month of excavating and $250,000 before motorists once again traveled over the Kirkland Creek Bridge without so much as a glance or being aware of the improvements.

CAMBRIDGE — As cities and industries grow, so do energy demands. Beneath the highways, rivers and fields of southern Ontario, a complex network of pipelines feed our need for heat and power. This 48-inch (1.3 m) diameter gas pipeline runs just south of Cambridge, and is capable of supplying the daily heat for 1.5 million residential homes. In the moment of construction there is a sense of upheaval, the land torn of its cover. Yet within a year the grass will return, crops will be seeded, and little evidence will remain of this intrusion.

RIVERVIEW — A first glance suggests Riverview qualifies as a "If you blink you'll miss it" kind of town. Eighty-four residents, not counting dogs and cats, live here, most of them commuters. But there was another time. The central white building is built on the foundation of the Bluebird Dance Hall, once known as "Little Chicago," the sort of place where mothers hesitated to have their daughters go on Saturday night. For years, people whooped it up with country music and smuggled-in beer. Sadly, the hall burned in 1948. But this hamlet still retains the distinction of being one of the northern-most communities on the upper Grand.

DUNDALK — All things end or, shifting perspective, all things begin. On a flight north, this is my last positive identification of the Grand River. Just north of Dundalk, the narrow stream splits and vanishes into a small woods. But as I turn south, I now see the river as emerging — two streams trickling together and birthing a new river. If I dropped a toy rubber ducky here, it would take seven days to complete its 185 mile (298 km) journey to the river's mouth at Port Maitland on Lake Erie.

PUNKEYDOODLE'S CORNERS — An alternative name for this place, located just south of New Hamburg, might be Convoluted Corners. Neither roads nor explanations run straight in this hamlet, with arguably Ontario's most amusing place name. Should Punkeydoodle's Corners be spelled as two words or one? With or without an apostrophe? Did the name really originate from the antics of innkeeper John Zurbuchen? Legend says that one night, Zurbuchen was boozily belting out "Yankee Doodle Went to Town." Somehow, the combination of beer and a thick accent resulted in "Punkey Doodle vent to town," and the name has stuck ever since.

KITCHENER — Leonard Missone, the great Belgian photographer of the 1930s often said. "Le sujet n'est rien. La lumiere c'est tout." (The subject is nothing. The light is all). The statement is extreme but defines many strong images. Rarely would a highway possess visual merit in my viewfinder. The exception happens only because of lighting. Just before sunset, the almost horizontal rays suddenly transform Homer Watson Blvd. into a dazzling ribbon of light. I would have never predicted this enchantment.

KITCHENER — Ski junkies tend not to take Chicopee ski hill seriously with its small, 200-foot (65 metres) vertical drop. But its operators are hardly apologetic. This is the only ski hill within the Grand River watershed and is ideally situated within the city.

Most significant, it is home to arguably the most successful "Track 3" program in all of Canada. More than 200 volunteer instructors assist about 100 mentally and physically challenged people to carve the slopes. In the words of one paraplegic skier, "I came full of fear, I persevered, and now I ski beyond the possibilities."

GLEN ALLAN — We motorists occasionally see snowmobiles waiting to cross our highways. Snowmobilers tolerate our passing as they glide through nearly 50,000 kilometres of surprise-packed Ontario trails. The network is amazingly sophisticated with direction signs, posted speed limits, and clubhouses enroute. Cambridge effectively defines the southern boundary of this short-lived, but intense winter sport. Even with a wind-chill factor of –75 C, the use of a full leather suit, heated handlebars and an adventurous spirit allow riders to blast comfortably into the very heart of winter.

GLEN ALLAN — They are increasingly rare, but it's still possible to find a quiet, sleepy hamlet where you don't drive into town when you run out of sugar, you just ask the neighbours. More than 100 years ago, the Guelph Herald newspaper claimed: "Nowhere is the world so gracious as between the green hills which encompass the Village of Glen Allan. One comes upon this lovely spot quite unawares." Little has changed. For the 150 residents who live here, the laid-back pace and the adjacent Conestogo Lake and River make it just about the perfect place to be.

YORK — Mention of the Grand River watershed likely brings to mind the main Grand itself, plus major tributaries such as the Conestogo, Nith, Speed and Eramosa. The surprise was discovering a proliferation of smaller creeks and streams. There is a hardly a square kilometre found anywhere in the Grand River watershed which does not have at least one creek flowing through it, with least-known names like Four Mile, Alder, Barlow, and Holmes. The total shoreline miles of all the Grand's lakes, rivers and streams has been calculated at 15,000 miles (22,000 km), the approximate equivalent of crossing Canada four times.

WASHINGTON — Isolated cemeteries lie scattered throughout the country, their once attendant churches having long disappeared. Discovering these markers of another time triggers both curiosity and reflection for me. Who were those people, what were their lives? Did they have fun? And what of my own mortality? Do I live my life with passion, with intention? Do I make a difference, does my life matter? I think also of my own epitaph, written several years ago in a contemplative moment. It came from boyhood memories of being the first to leap from a diving board into the creek...now a simple metaphor to be fully in this world: "C'mon in, the water's great."

ALMA — When Carol Geddes sits in her favourite pew — right side, three rows from the back — and looks around the church, she smiles with a familiar comfort. Around her are five generations of the Scott family. In May 2003, Grandfather Douglas turned 95, while her grandson Blair is just two. Both Douglas' father and grandfather helped build St. Andrew's Presbyterian Church way back in 1893. With a new steel roof and a commitment to on-going restoration, St. Andrew's will likely provide the Scott family a place of worship for years to come.

St. Clements

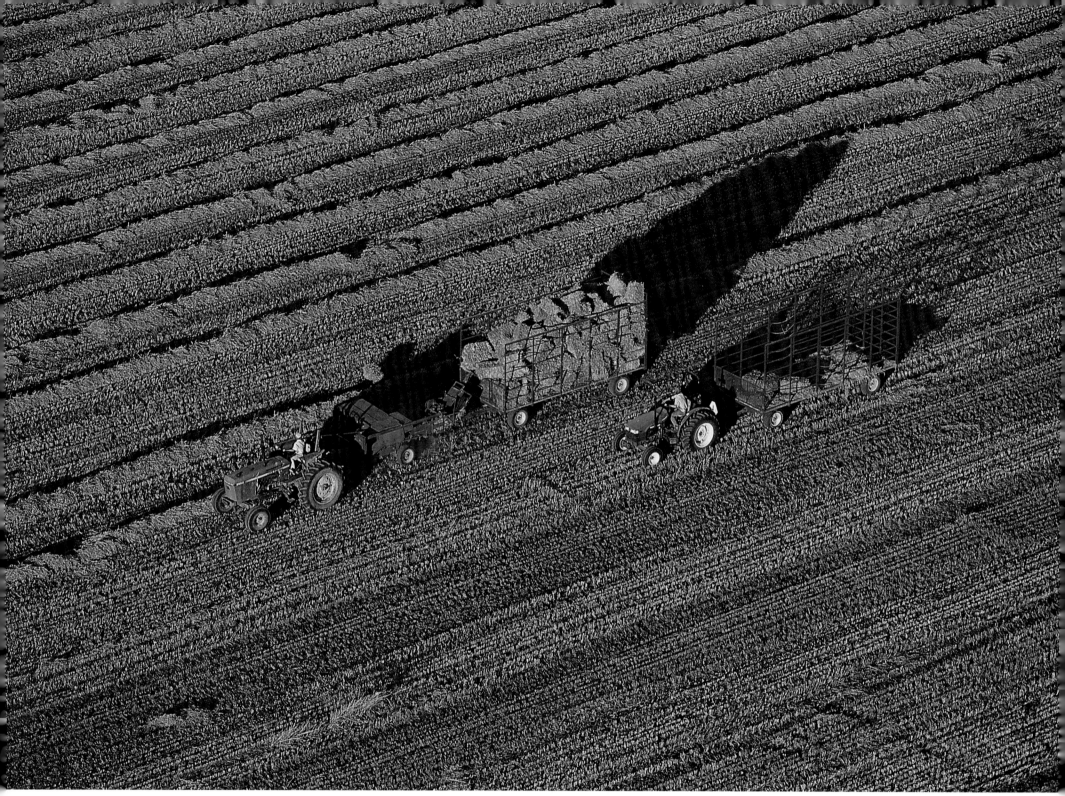

ST. CLEMENTS & INVERHAUGH — There is a juxtaposition of farming technologies found in Waterloo Region unlike anywhere else in Canada. These photographs could have been taken on the same flight, over adjacent fields. Conservative Mennonite and Amish farmers, on their typical 100-acre (41 hectare) farms, understand hard work and traditional farming practices to be virtuous, a way of being separate from the world. A progressive neighbour spends huge capitalization dollars, trying to reduce the workload and enabling him to farm ever larger acreages. Yet they co-exist easily, respecting their differing philosophies.

BELWOOD LAKE — In 1942, the builders of the Shand Dam had no idea how far-reaching their project would become. It was the first dam ever constructed in Canada solely for water conservation purposes. Dams were historically seen as a source for hydro or water power, but the Shand both reduced spring flooding and added river water during the dry summer months. The showcase venture eventually became the catalyst for the creation of conservation authorities throughout Ontario.

GRAND VALLEY — For years I assumed the hydro transmission lines dissecting our country simply linked a power source to consumers nearby. The reality is a network grid of enormous complexity. Ontario's major generation stations, like the ones at Niagara (hydro), Nanticoke (coal) and Bruce (nuclear), all feed into a central grid. In turn, it's part of a much larger web-like network crossing the borders of Quebec, the U.S., and the western provinces. Electricity can flow either way depending on supply, demand, and pricing, and whether we are importing or exporting at a given time.

WALLENSTEIN — A careful look at this farmyard lends insight into Mennonite farm life. The house is larger than it appears. Grandparents live in the *doddy haus*, partially hidden by trees, as part of a three-generation household. There are also young children, for a green fence defines their outdoor play yard. A huge double barn includes the "straw barn," where a traditional threshing machine has blown in piles of loose straw. Beef cattle crowded under the open-roof shed, as well as extensive fencing, denote this as a cattle operation. On the extreme left, a wood pile is the winter's heat source. The details go on. How much would we learn, looking at a house, in a typical subdivision?

ORTON — "Yeah, they call me Smoky now," laughs Rick, "but it didn't seem so funny then." The front brake on Rick's combine heated up, ignited a handful of chaff and within minutes, fire swept through the 125 acre (50 hectare) wheat field. But good luck also smiled that day. Swept by dry summer winds, the fire blew itself away from the buildings (middle right of picture) and into the forest where it soon self-extinguished. Even farmers have quotas on how much excitement they need for one day.

CAYUGA — It all started one Saturday night, in the early 1930s. Local resident Blake Humfries claimed his Grey Dort car was so powerful that farmer friend Cal Williamson couldn't budge it with his tractor. The bet was on and townspeople were soon hysterical as the tractor's wheels spun helplessly in the dirt. The next weekend, unable to pass on a good laugh, 20 farmers on foot pulled the same tractor backwards down the street. The crowd loved it and the astute town fathers began organizing regular Saturday night events. But the party really got going when microphone and speakers were rigged to a hand-cranked Victrola record player, and a great street dance evolved. Cayuga soon became known throughout Southern Ontario as the place to kick up your heels on a Saturday night. The outbreak of war in 1939 ended an era about which old timers still fondly reminisce.

DUNNVILLE — There are more sides to a dam than simply above and below. Cottagers, anglers and recreational boaters clearly benefit from the larger waterways. Yet environmentalists and biologists see another side. Because of older mill and navigation dams, no lake sturgeon have been able to reach their traditional breeding grounds up the Grand since 1832. Water temperatures are higher while oxygen deprivation lowers the quality. Dams can trap sediment flowing from upstream and, over the years, reduce the usable habitat. Finding the balance in this delicate equation is an on-going challenge.

GOBLES — A cross-country pilot navigating over Southern Ontario learns one lesson quickly. You do not rely on the supposed gridwork predictability of our roadways. For that, early surveyors can be thanked. New surveys often used shorelines of rivers and lakes as their initial reference points. The work was a long continual process, further complicated by each township setting its own pattern. In some instances, the results were completely haphazard. At least here the intersecting side road has been straightened to give approaching drivers a clearer, safer view.

BADEN — Who was the first aviator who soared high enough to suddenly discover his own rainbow-held shadow skipping along the cloud tops? The phenomenon, a "glory" or "pilot's rainbow," is caused by sunlight reflecting from the cloud's water droplets. Mountaineers commandeering a summit at sunrise or sunset could experience the same effect, as would skydivers in free-fall, blasting into the clouds at 120 mph (180 kph).

WELLESLEY — The simple elements of this photograph belie the difficulty of taking it. I had only one chance, and had to get it right within a few seconds. The challenge was one of relative motion. It was easy to spot the bus on its predictable travel toward the bridge. I circled, about three fields away, my brain racing, trying to determine the precise moment I should angle out toward the bridge to time my arrival with that of the crossing bus. Sometimes, planning and a bit of luck make it all come together.

HEIDELBERG — The back roads of Waterloo Region are a lure for bicyclists and joggers alike. Find a quiet concession at sunrise and you'll just as likely hear the nostalgic clip-clop of a horse and buggy as the roar of a passing truck. Distinctive to this area are the extra wide shoulders of most roads, allowing safer passage for the Mennonites and their alternative transportation.

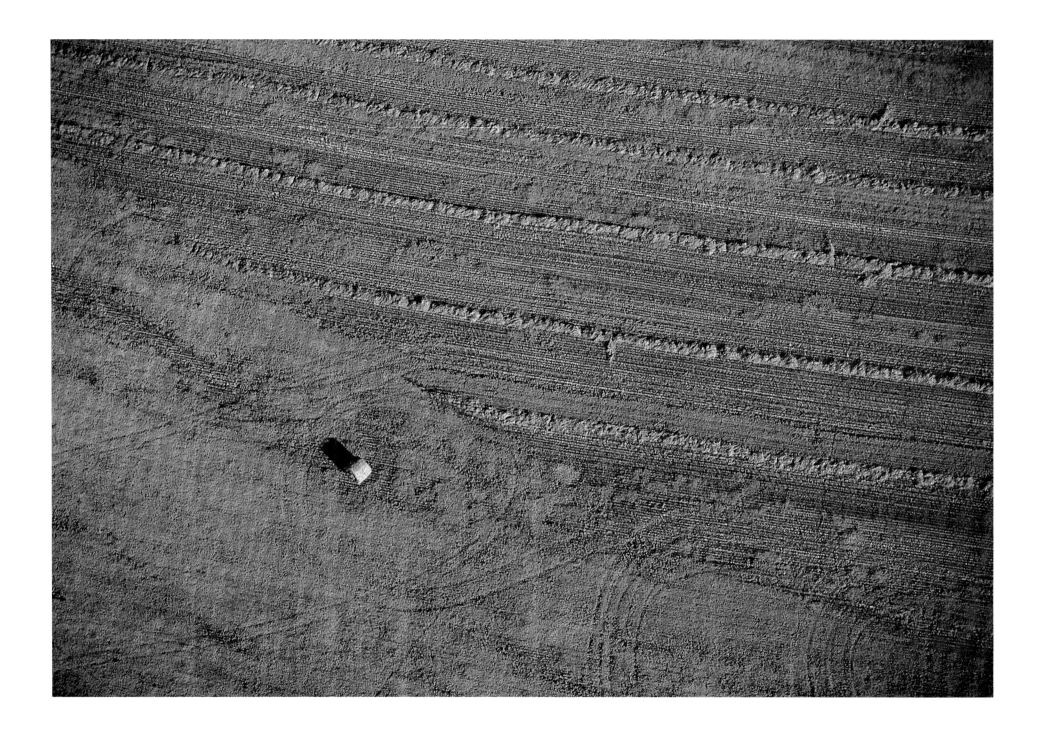

YORK — Painters and photographers share similarities and differences in their work. Artists begin with a blank canvas while photographers face a full viewfinder. One adds the detailed elements while the other often does their best work as a reductionist. This field was littered with round hay bales and a carpet of green weeds angled through the decaying swaths. I sensed immediately the image I wanted to bring home, but it took numerous passes and half a roll of film to isolate this lone bale and frame it in the corner.

NEW HAMBURG — Not uncommonly, New Hamburg has virtually become a town within a town. Its Victorian core, now defined as a Heritage Conservation District, reflects a time when street greetings were by first name and the post-office was as much a place to catch up on the news as to retrieve mail. Today, new subdivisions ringing the town contain over half the total population. Older residents carry a quiet regret for a time that used to be.

BRANTFORD — John Wyskiel's son rolled his eyes and faked horror when his dad told him of his new plant manager's job at Canadian Blue Bird Coach Lines. "You mean the place that makes those nasty things that take you to school each day?" The company produces about 6,000 buses annually. By the middle of August, awaiting pickup for the new school season, 900 or more units are lined up in the parking lots. Any normal school child would be overwhelmed.

WELLESLEY — Today's average Canadian changes jobs six times and moves numerous times during a lifetime. Brian Jantzi wonders why. He is the fourth generation on this 234-acre (95 hectare) family dairy farm, and never doubts this is where he belongs. His wife Cindy concurs. "When I walk out the side door in the morning and see and smell my garden, I just feel content and blessed." As I flew past this calendar-perfect scene I could understand their connection and love for the land.

WELLESLEY — City children think cows are cute, kinda goofy, have big eyes, and are so embarrassing when "they go to the bathroom right in front of you." The dairy farmer, watching his herd for years, is amazed by their habits and smarts. "When it's milking time, they usually know within 15 minutes when to head for the barn. But what really amazes me," says Darcy Weber, "is how they can distinguish between a short and long rain shower. If it's raining while they're feeding in the morning, and they stay inside, you know it's going to be a short rain. If they leave, it will likely rain all day. They must figure they have to leave sometime and if it's going to rain all day anyway, 'Let's just get it over with.'"

BRANTFORD — Winter changes everything for the aerial photographer. Fields of vibrant, contrasting colours have been harvested, strangled by frost, buried under furrows or layers of snow. With the odd exception, summer's extravagant palette is reduced to a simpler design of black and white. But the beauty now resides in unexpected places where form dominates colour in a more graphic world. It feels perhaps like learning to see through new eyes.

BRANTFORD — In a letter to his future wife, Alexander Graham Bell wrote of taking a rug and pillow to a cozy nook beside the river to "dream away the afternoon in luxurious idleness." Bell later described his dreaming place as the birthplace of "talking electricity," the world's most significant patented invention and the site of the first-ever long-distance phone call, which was made from Paris to Brantford. Sadly, years of erosion have removed the dreaming place but the Bell Homestead and property still proudly convey a sense of this great man and his invention.

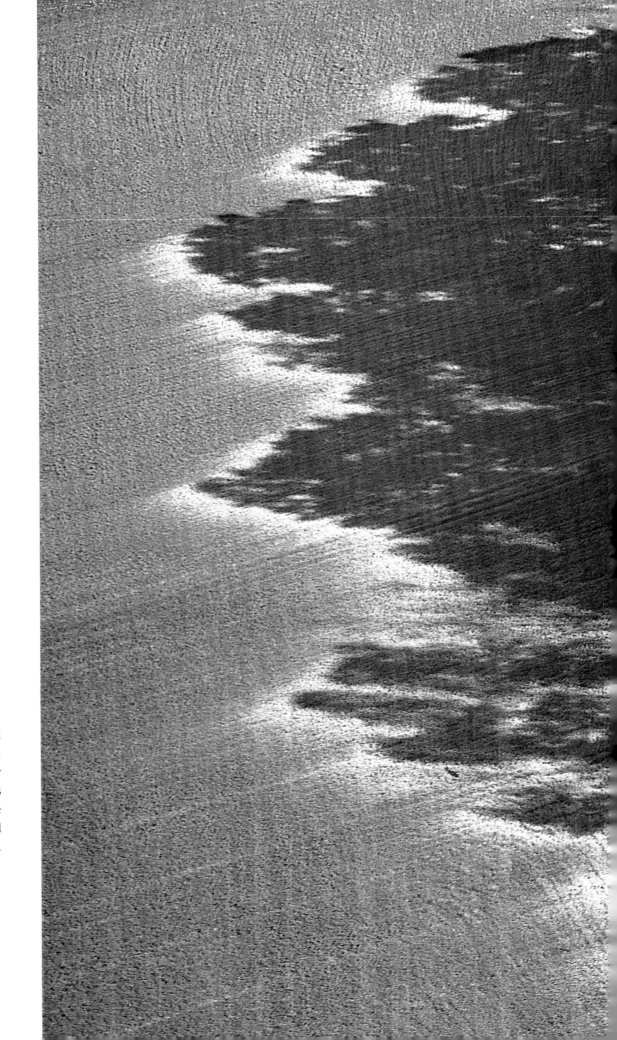

ST. AGATHA — Nature is a prolific painter, with fall colours emerging from her extravagant brush strokes. A closer look reveals more subtle art. A cold October morning has frosted the fields white. But the painting is neither static nor complete. Even as I circle overhead, the sun continues its work, slowly herding the frost-rimmed shadow back into the forest. In an hour, it will be gone.

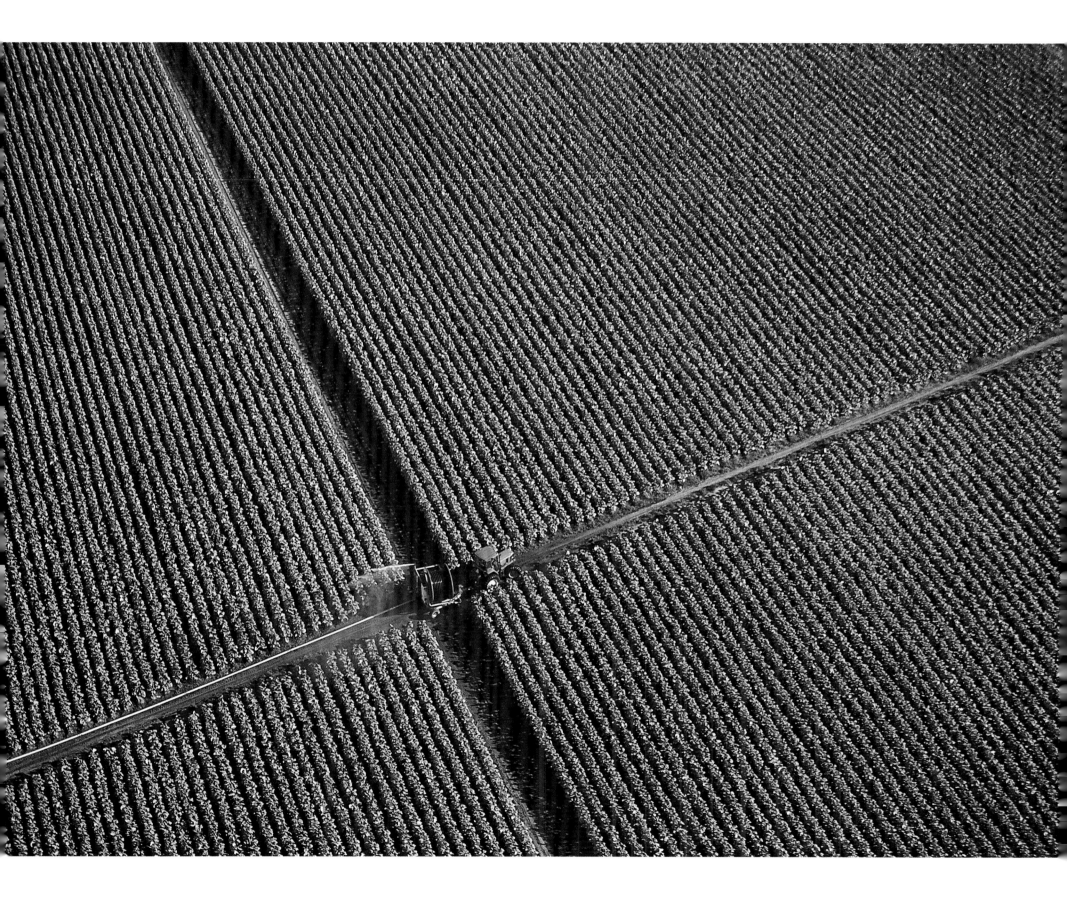

SCOTLAND — The shift in Canadian smoking habits reflects a radical social change. In the early 1960s, approximately half of our population smoked. Today, that number has fallen to only 22%, thanks to tireless education programs and strong policy measures. What has been welcome news for health care professionals and anti-smoking lobbyists, however, has been a difficult transition for tobacco farmers in Southern Ontario. Today, they grow less than half the amount of tobacco of earlier years, diverting many of their fields to vegetables and highly specialized crops such as ginseng.

PARIS — What's in a name? It took a Yankee entrepreneur, Hiram Capron, to put Paris on the map. At the confluence of the Nith and Grand Rivers, Hiram discovered local deposits of gypsum — used initially as a fertilizer, and today in construction materials. This, he thought, would make an ideal village site. Since Paris, France, had similar gypsum deposits along the Seine, borrowing the name seemed a logical leap. And how many tradesmen think of the town's name today when they mix their plaster-of-paris slurries?

PARIS — Mike MacDougal is one of a handful of men in Canada who specialize in high tower maintenance. When he summits the 1,000 foot (300 m) TVO/CBC transmission tower near Paris, there is no special danger pay, even though the work is often completed at night. With a rubber flashlight clamped in his mouth, and tied off with a safety rope, Mike is as comfortable here as in his office chair. His one memorable experience was falling 15 feet, breaking a leg, and then hopping down the remaining 300 feet (95 m) on his other leg. All this, nine days before his wedding. "No problem" laughed Mike, "They painted the cast black so it matched my tuxedo."

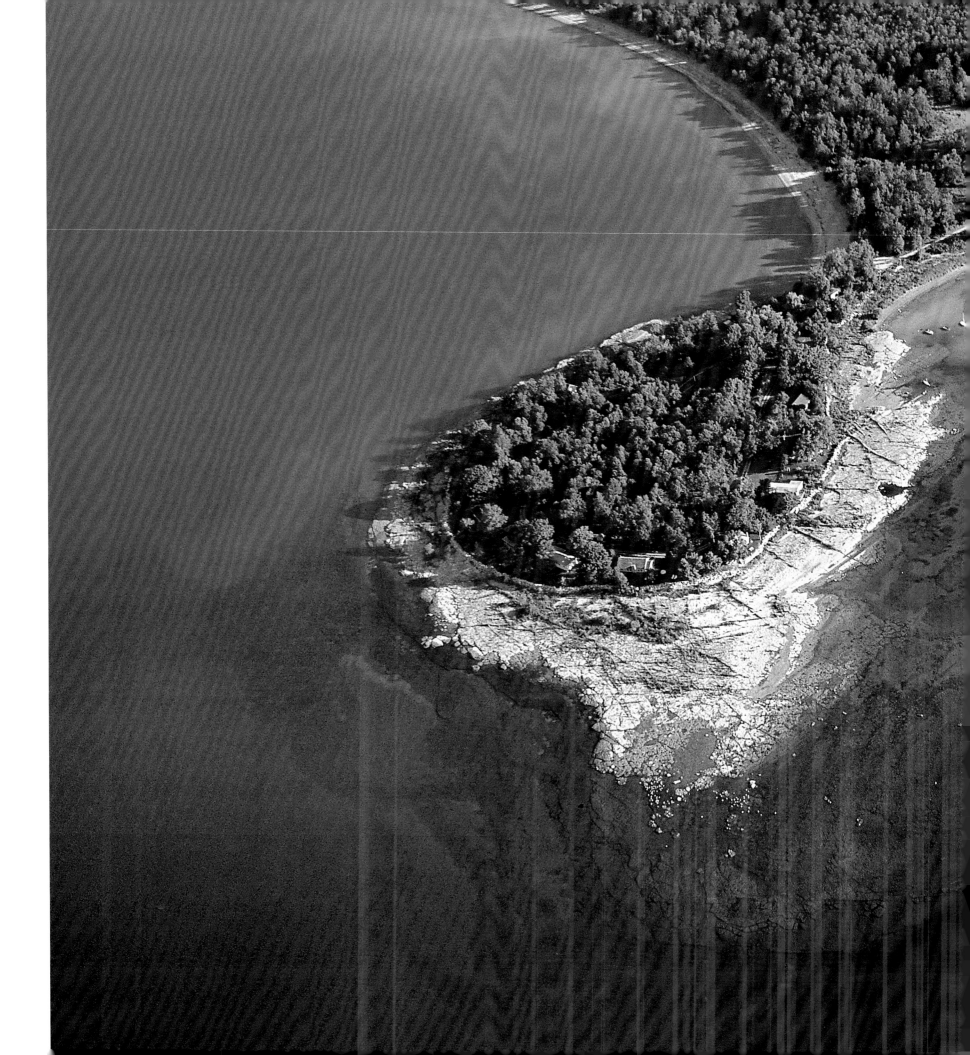

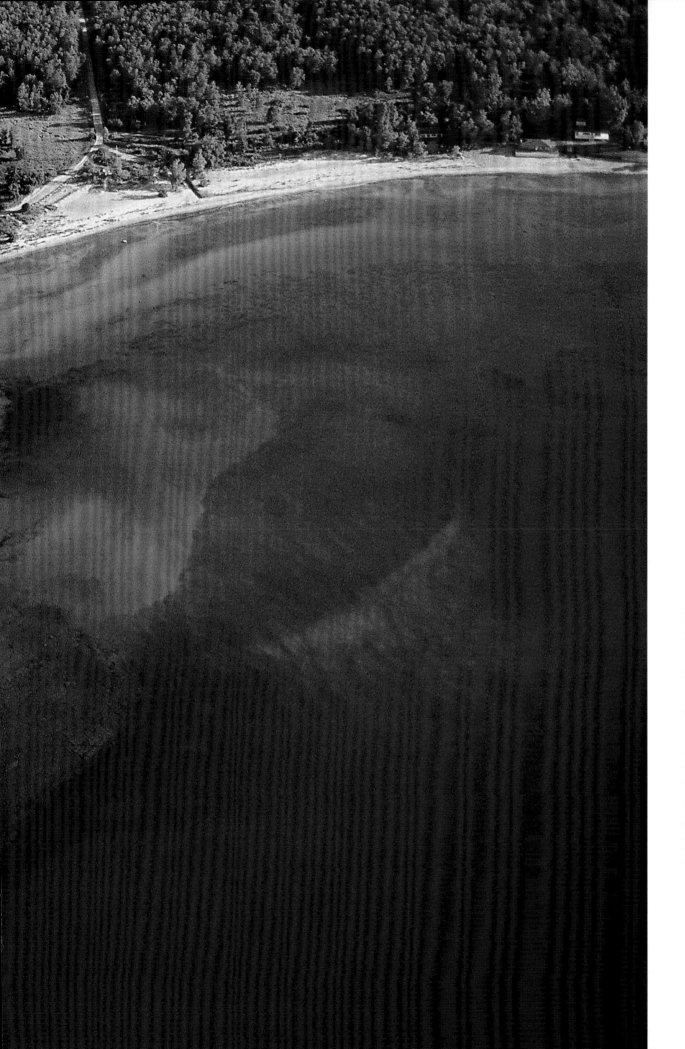

LOW POINT — One might easily despise zebra mussels. Since their invasion of the Great Lakes in the mid-1980s, most likely brought here in ballast from an ocean freighter, they have clogged water intake lines, encrusted boat hulls and sliced the feet of unsuspecting bathers like new razor blades. Yet they return a simple gift. Zebra mussels are filter feeders. Every day, each one filters about one litre of water. It is estimated the entire lake is cleansed the equivalent of at least once each week. The result is a water clarity not seen in 50 years. Scuba divers delight in discovering shipwrecks, while I am privileged to view the rock base of this peninsula as it slides off into the swirling depths.

DUNNVILLE — *Dunnville's history has always been closely tied to the river. In the early 1820s, the first step in building a diversionary waterway to feed the newly-constructed Welland Canal was to dam the river at Dunnville. Workmen poured into the village and soon transformed it into "Slabtown" as they hastily constructed their slabwood houses. The dam has been rebuilt several times since. And for years to come, children will likely continue spending their lazy days of summer here, fishing lines bobbing in the spillway, thoughts lost in the endless flow of the river.*

GRAND RIVER CONSERVATION FOUNDATION

The Grand River Conservation Foundation was incorporated in 1965 (as the Grand Valley Conservation Foundation) as a registered, charitable, non-profit organization. Its volunteers from communities throughout the Grand River watershed raise funds to support local and tangible environmental projects. The Foundation's primary object is to raise funds for projects of the Grand River Conservation Authority which cultivate and advance conservation in the Province of Ontario.

In turn, the Grand River Conservation Authority is a partnership of watershed municipalities and the Province of Ontario. Its major aim is the management of natural resources within the valley of the Grand, for the benefit of all watershed residents.

As a project of the Foundation, it is intended that the publishing of *The Grand River — An Aerial Journey* fulfill two key goals:

First, it will provide readers with a personal view of the watershed, thus opening up the Grand's landscapes, unique geographic features, cities and historic sites to their own personal paths of discovery,

Second, as a fund-raising vehicle, all profits from the sale of this book will be used to forward the Foundation's objectives. In the past, the Foundation has supported the Conservation Authority in the establishment of nature centre facilities and outdoor education programs, wildlife habitat improvement, fisheries enhancement, native tree species reintroduction, the acquisition of environmentally sensitive lands, and the development of scenic Rail-Trails and related outdoor recreation facilities.

Further information concerning the programs of the Grand River Conservation Foundation
may be obtained by contacting the Foundation's offices at (519) 621-2761 in Cambridge,
by email to: foundation@grandriver.ca or on the website at www.grandriver.ca.